T0142434

EXPECT THE BEST NEVER SETTLE FOR LESS

Words of Encouragement and Poems!

Azell Edwards

authorHOUSE®

AuthorHouse™
1663 Liberty Drive
Bloomington, IN 47403
www.authorhouse.com
Phone: 1 (800) 839-8640

Published by AuthorHouse 03/22/2016

ISBN: 978-1-5049-8360-0 (sc)
ISBN: 978-1-5049-8359-4 (e)

Print information available on the last page.

Life is precious because most people reading this is alive. just kidding we all are alive. It's truly a blessing that out of many cells we beat the odds and came into this world. most of us miss that fact everyday when we look at this world and say i have nothing to give to it. and why should i succeed? Life kicks us all around in the butt but it's the way we get up that defines us. No one likes the fight but it's the win that makes the pain acceptable. Each person has a skill talent or God given ability to shape, change, or innovate the world like we never seen before. It's your goal as a human to find purpose in life and fight til you're dead to acheive it. Then take that gift and make the world anew with that gift from God. From helping your neighbors, to surviving wars and serving our country. use that gift to help people take their problems away in this crazy world in a song.

This is your time to shine like the sun. For a person that wants to or thinks about committing suicide this is for you, The main reason you are here is to help someone that is in the same pain as you are. you're not alone hold tight and let the universe find you for your purpose. If you leave here the person you could have helped is lost. Everyone has purpose. The family you leave behind and conflict the pain on could help you and you can be healed. If not family friends a good buddy or spouse can be there in your time of need. The void you leave makes the world sad because you take the gift you have to the grave with you. Besides you could live another day and win the lottery.

How about a future new mate or friends or invent that new gizmo. All is lost when you decide to end your life. tho you might be depressed or feel no one cares there is someone out there that does God, your mom, your pet's me. Find your divine destiny in the universe by holding on and riding this horse called life till you are called home by natural causes.

You're not alone tho you may think you are but it's a lots of people that think like you and stick it out. Sit down and write yourself and say i may be at ropes end but my best days of life are in ahead of me. New trips and a world to see. And even if i'm poor i can always be the best and talk about the problem with my family, friends, or someone I can trust. If i'm rich no problem or worries are too big for God. Put that money to good use and help a kid or senior that struggles to makes ends meet. Your be blessed and the universe will bless you with good Karma.

Part Two In order to live in a world with so many different personalities you have to have a thick skin and have God on your shoulders to lean on because people will take you there. The best way to deal with that is to meditate or take a walk or go to the bathroom and clear your mind. My favorite is to count until i stop being upset or i stop being angry when i think to myself is this worth being angry all day and the answer is no, When you do that it relieves stress and you total forget what you were mad about in the first place.

Most of the time the person that snaps at you has the same stress as you have. It just that they can't handle it in a proper way. On those kinds of situations it's better if you smile or have a funny comeback not insults either. But something that will make a person think why did I snap at them in the first place. 90% of the time it works but you have that 10% that no matter what you do they will always be mad until God calls them home for eternal rest. You can't do anything about that. Just make sure you do the right thing so Karma gives you a star for your good effort. I always say it's better to spread love than to join the bitter crew of life and make every one's life a bowl full of lemons. I got asked all the time Why do you smile all the time and i say it's because in this world we got enough people that Frowning and contributing to the grumpy crew. When you smile as the quote says the whole world smiles at you. And in fact i truly believe that. Most people want to be loved and respected. Now for me the three things that i can't live without and that is love, happiness and making people feel good and happy and a sense of worth. If we had more of that the world would be less war like and more peaceful. Happyness is where you make it.

Whether you're in the delta of the south or on the southside of Chicago, you have to make sure you're happy at least 90% of your life. There will be bills, Kids and stress that will make you lose your mind but the key is to stay focus and know that you are in a dark place but you don't have to stay there. you'll be at a job that the people will hate you. Or in situations where you deserve a raise and get none. Keep doing your best. It may take days, months or even years but know that God is on your side and Karma is your buddy.

You will get everything you want in time because you deserve it in the end and if you do your part of helping people biting your tongue when you want to go off and curse them out, Be the best person you can be to avoid it. Make this world better than you left it before you came into it. And people will say that you light up the place when your present was there. And you made people reflect on themselves to see how they can make their own light on the world, and universe.

Respect

Respect is God's love for a person. When we show love to each other it shows that we can have compassion for a person even if that person doesn't deserves it. It takes a lot of meditation and inner peace to not tell that person off. I've learned that the best way to win a person over is to show them kindness and love. Not just to receive something but the joy of doing the right thing.

When everything in your body is pointing to why should you it's them that did you wrong. But I never knew anyone that felt rewarded after telling someone off. In fact you feel worse because you later think you could have handled it differently. Our youth more now than ever need to learn this value. In the streets so many of our youth feel disrespected. They result in using a gun to solve a problem because they feel disrespected. But later on they learn the hard way that their problems are just beginning because of their choice. Its for us to teach them to cool down and walk away. In that choice you save two lives, The gunman and the victim. it's a lack of the elders to talk to these young mind as the elders did when i was a child and growing up here in Chicago. I was taught to respect my elders. No cursing in front of them. get your lazy butt up on the bus when you see a older person that needs a seat or pregnant lady. Stop to offer and help a person with too many bags into their car or home or on the bus.

Always pick up your date from her parents home or work if you're going on a date, And on a first date a woman should never pay. NEVER! Always pray and thank God for the little things so you can be blessed with bigger things. Obey your parents even if they are fussing and an apology even if you think your right. Never compromise your beliefs for no one and put God first in every decision you make because that the best place next to your parents or grandparents. Work hard on any job or school because that builds merit, Also stay positive when you are struggling because you will rise in the end. Respect is your name and you wear it proudly. You young readers never call each other names or cuss or disrespect a lady or when a lady is by you. You are a child of God not a hoe, slut, or bitch. Young ladies never stoop to that level to call each other that. You're a child of God and a queen nothing less. Stand tall no matter what color you are and know you are here for a reason not just to waste your life on doing nothing find your purpose and go for it. Dress nice with your parents and your mate and not with your pants hanging down. you are better than that. Dress like the guys in the 50's 60's 70's and 80's those guys and women knew how to dress for success and always made it.

Encouragement

I can't tell you how important it is to encourage someone. whether they are having a bad day or just need to see a smile. Your action makes the difference between someone killing a group of people or them putting down the gun and praying with you. I feel that we as human being need to be encourage in life. To achieve a goal to work thru a marriage or relationship or someone to lean on in good times and bad, It's that boost our spirit and give us a jolt of God's love and we as human being need to do that everyday to a stranger, the manger, the boss, or kid who has not a dad or mom. The teacher that cares about our kids enough to work with them instead of passing the blame of failure to the child and parents, We are all in this together no me or i just we working together for God's greater good and purpose. i feel when i talk to a child it's like god's helping hand to show the way. It's not a day that goes by that we shouldn't be doing that. I do it all the time with my nephew and nieces they are the future of this world and we better uplift them and teach them to have compassion on homeless people the poor and the sick and shut in. Churches do that as well as salvation army. But we can do it too. No not looking for a reward but the honor of helping someone as Jesus would do.

My best encouragement is my mom. she been thru a lot but always had time to encourage someone to talk about the bible or tell someone that it's going to get better and the rain will pass over. She raised us on little but gave us a lot my sister and i. Never talk negative about our circumstances and all ways told us that we can achieve whatever we wanted too but always put God first and the rest will come. Never be doubtful or believe in failures but know the best is in us and we will bring it out as God is ready for your season. My goal is to teach people that God is here and loves us but we have to see it first. It's not in a bottle or drugs or money or anything negative but your faith in God and the ability to see beyond that crack house or the gun shots by your windows. It's in you to see it and achieve it. To strive and survive to show the world what you're made of. You're the best show the world you are.

Life

In causing sin don't hurt people by talking about them then smile in their face. you cause more damage by crushing the person heart and stabbing them in the back. So many friendships, family and relationship have fallen because of the words of a viper tongue. The best rule is if you have nothing good to say about a person don't say anything at all. You can do a great work in uplifting people and giving them a positive word or compliment than being negative or down on them. I see a many parents do that to a child. You slowly killed a person inside doing that. Always smiles before frowns. In life there are struggles times when you ask God why am i going thru this but in those time you have to look at the bigger picture and see that your better days are ahead of you.

Ups and downs victory and loss it's those that say that life will kick you at the worst time but in those times that builds you up and makes you the hero you will become. I success is what you have to believe in. That's not a typo i meant that sentence. you are a success and only i you will be in control with God's help. You are the best and no one can take that away from you. You be your own cheerleader when you have none and you see your dream when you have no help or everyone says you can't do that it's impossible.

Block out negative thoughts or negative people because those are dreams killers. You can be your own worst enemy if you believe that crap and let it come into your soul. you keep on pushing and succeeding because you deserve it. Work hard never take short cuts and respect and honor the people that made the way. But in all you do never i mean never forget God in your success. stay true to yourself and never be too big to help someone, sign an autograph or take time to give God you time in the day.

Poems

Loyalty

Depend on God with your heart and soul. Leave your problems
and worries by the Garbage can.

Only you can save yourself
with the help of God!

Remember to help your friend or enemy

because one day the favor may be return

to you.

Always smiles because the heavens smiled
on you today!!!

In life there are two paths,
Your destiny and the life you
 live.

Poems

Be bound by truth
because it will take you far.

Love by the soul not with the mind!

Two hearts can never be broken with true enlightenment.

**Faith is firm as a rock and is
 strong as a storm.**

Let your soul shine like the kingdom of
heaven in all its glory

A real father is a blessing to his children and a model for the world.

A mother's love can never be broken,
thru life or death or the troubles of the
times. She will hold firm to her journey.

A man strength is his love of blessed hope and peace.

The ways of the world are not yours, choose wisely

The sounds of children are a whisper from
God!

In moments in time you can hear the world cry
not because of war and strife but the joy of life
reborn.

To hold your hand soft as a blanket in a cradle.

Your love flows each part of my heart keeping
me alive

The burst of your smile touches me so everly
brightly.

Being near you is a delight to know your in my
soul

FOREVER MORE!

As life beats you down you'll rise like the tide

with force and might, the world can't stop you,

your a force of one. Capable of rising and surviving

 the ride of life.

You are the best and never settle for short

you make you path and only God can judge you.

 glory awaits you in your sea of success.

Us Vs. Aliens Vs. Zombies

April fools day, Goliath Edwards is riding the train home when the lights started to blink on the train. It was a routine day at first, grab my donuts from my favorite spot and head up to the train before it leaves. its packed and i hadn't had a decent bite to eat all day. The smells of babies and pee filled the air. My return to chicago is as just as adventurous as the days in the military. the train rocked back and forward as always then a loud whooping sound is heard. The people begin to fall all over the train. In slow motion people are screaming and i catch the baby as he is falling out the stroller. Then the train stopped! My first thought is to run to see if everyone else is ok and see if the conductor is ok? So i run between cars and its hectic,

People are still screaming and to my surprise the conductor was in a daze. I asked him was he ok and he look at me and pointed and the missing wall and these things were eating the people on the platform and i looked at him. come on this is a joke right? but then i saw that thing bust through a concrete wall thick enough to hold fort knock in. The conductor asked me what are those things i looked at him and said the hell i know. Before i could say another word the thing busted the side door open and tried to get us, I took the fire extinguisher and spray it then hit that thing with all i had and it slumped over and we ran out the subway with the rest of the people. I looked into the sky and it was Alien ships by the hundreds, All over the city.

Those ships were as big as soldiers field. My mind raced and i had to call home.

My mother answered. She asked me what was going on. The military had the whole city on lockdown and the mayor was giving a press conference. Everyone thought it was a big joke at first but it was very real. I told her to stay in the house and i would be there soon. Running down state street people are in a panic the military is shooting people are getting caught in the crossfire, The thing are taking out tanks its a mess. The big mother ship start to shoot out pods like hershey kisses. they hit the ground and more of those thing come out.

I grab a gun left behind and take out as many as i can. As the soldiers move in it's a heated battle and the things re-treat. But it's a bloody mess on the streets with alien and human bodies everywhere, I see my mom's house and one of those things burst out of one of the remaining pods and grabs me by the neck and tries to bite my head off i aim the gun towards its mouth and fire blue blood goes everywhere, I see they go down like everyone else. I finally make it to the house and in the sky you can see f16 firing at the mother ship. She fires back and disintegrate the plane with one streak of light into dust.

I knocked on the door hard mom open up it's me She comes to the door with a alien head. mom looked at me and said he was messing with my cooking time. On the tv in the living room my family is watching some are crying. my uncle says see it's the end of the world. I knew better tho. I saw the same thing, it's not that! He says it is! the Horseman just not the horses but spaceships. I laugh and I told mom please put that head thing outside. She said it's going on my fireplace after this is over, I get a call from my old seal leader. We need you back, come at once. So i hug the family and told them to stay inside the house until this is over. Drive out the garage and head back into downtown. Those pods were everywhere. martial law is in effect. But something stop my car dead in its tracks. I tried to go in reverse and it wouldn't move and forward nothing then it happen. Being trapped by this alien creature. I had only two options. One take him out or two see what he was up to and then get him. But he surprised me by saying this. I have no intentions of harming you.

I want peace in both of these galaxies and to restore this planet back to where it was before the invasion. I'm here on a peace mission not to kill but to save life forces here and the universe. This kat just read my mind. so i had no choice but to take him to the general and let him in on this. so the military is out and about shooting every alien in sight. I thought he would get out and either kill them for killing his people or eat them. He looked at me and said them brought that on themselves your warriors are just protecting themselves, and our race doesn't eat people. I told him you gotta stop reading my mind.

As we pulled up to the military base two soldiers point m-16 at the car. I put my hands and yelled the mayor and the general are expecting me. The alien said please whatever you do don't let them take me if they find out i'm an alien. I've been studying earth life and i know they will take me after this and experiment on me and use my planets knowledge for evil. even if i was to save this planet. I wouldn't care but we both know better. I went to shake his hand and his tongue came out. I'm sorry but that how we agree on things on our planet. I laughed he had a sense of humor. he smiled and said let's save you planet. kdbn {kabon} is his name and my new friend never in a million years i thought i would ever say that.

So we are escorted to the basement where there are so many scientific and military you think you were in washington dc. The professor is explaining to me that a wormhole open up and the aliens appeared. Kabon stepped in and said we make our own what you call wormholes to travel to the galaxy we want. they looked at him and i had to pull him to the side don't tell them that they will use that again your people and others. I had to clean it up for him he was joking he means that how they arrived and he's an expert on alien life. The professor asked him what school did he come from? He boldly said the university of yale and the professor looked stunned and said welcome aboard.

Kabon told them the aliens are like them but hate extreme heat regular temperatures are fine but radioactive like microwaves will kill us i meant them if exposed too long. Everyone started to laugh professor K is the man. The two got to work on a weapon to stop the aliens and the next day the weapon was complete. I said when they test that thing will you be ok. he smiled and said i wear this wristband i'm the one who gave someone the ideal for the smart watch and he wink at me.

The military emailed and ciso every president and leader in the world about the prototype and soon the alien were taking mass losses they packed up and retreated. cheers went all around the planet. I looked at k and said they don't know an alien saved their planet. He smiled and said now i'm a us citizen. But what they did know was a new threat was a foot with all of that radioactive blaster spreading in the ground. the dead began to arise, mixed with the alien blood they began to come out the ground in hospitals and even on crime scene, Breaking news blast across the airwave. Dead reborn true judgement day. Then i get a called its from my uncle i told you and he hung up. I ask the professor what is going on. He said the radioactive juice kick started and the alien blood gave them life. Now people are in a panic again boarding houses and looting stores. These zombies don't just eat people they could think and react to danger.

They would eat a soldier and then take his weapon and shoot at the rest of the soldiers.

We never seen anything like it they keep coming. once again k and the professor had to figure out some way to stop them that meant we had to capture one and study it. I was like ok you have the same blood maybe we can use your blood to see how they work. K took a needle and took some of his blood and the professor walk in. my goodness you are one of those things!!! I step in front of them no he an alien but not the zombies walking around. He smiled and said i couldn't put down a friend but those zombies yes. we all laugh but i told them we have to keep this a secret so k life would not be in danger.

We worked around the clock until k yell in his native language i done it. what i said? All we have to do is make a reverse ray to split the radiation and my race d.n.a from these monsters. its like dialysis for zombies. We sat down and got on the conference monitor and told the president we had found a way to stop the zombie rampage. She said get to work so we did for three day and built the the lazer to fit on the jet. With it you could cover lots of ground and not miss too many. On the ground you make mini one that zap the life force out of them.

K, professor and i hit the streets and tested the mini packs. they stall at first and as the professor was about to be eaten k pushed him out the way and i acendetly hit him with the ray eposing his real skin and he was hurt. I panicked k oh God im im he looked at me and said its ok friend its part of war sometimes you get caught in the crossfire. it wasnt looking good for k. But the professor picked him up and said our friend will not die. so we drove to the base and The general was there is that k did he get bit. we played along and the professor put him in a chamber. He told me in this atmosphere he will die but back on his home planet he would heal faster if we could get him back. I yelled how?

He said to me he is my best friend and he told me secrets of the worm hole all we have to do is steal a space shuttle. I asked how are we going to do that? they are in florida! no he said its one here in chicago. lets go take that one and you know we may never be able to come back. But all he has done for us and this planet we have to do it. I agreed so we hid inside the museum til closing and then lowered the shuttle down and k said please leave me be and walk away you dont have to do this for me. But i looked at him and said I made you a promise not to let them test on you if they found out the truth and they will if you die here.

1. So K told us how to fix the ship and prepare us for the trip. I knew it may be a one way shot but he had done so much for us. i had to help my friend and then the security came. k made a forcefield to keep us safe from the bullets, and then the cops. The professor

said its time to go we open the roof and strapped in k. we looked at each other and the professor said if anyone wants to leave now do so. we all laugh and K hit the button and we shot out like a light into space. now the rest of our stories are told another day but i can say k made it but if there is a threat and you look in the sky know you got three friends that will save the day!

About the Author

Born July 1973 to southern parents Geneva and Azell Edwards sr. Attended john foster Dulles elementary school, William Shakespeare elementary school and Enrico Fermi elementary school. High school Englewood h.s. graduated in 1991 and attended Richard j. Daley college graduates with A. A. degree in 1997. Active with the first jurisdiction of Illinois in spreading the word of God to people at special places and season.

Why readers will be interested in your unique voice as a author. In life we all need a book of encouragement and uplifting words. Too many times we hear more negative than positive. So my book is for the times when you want your soul motivated or see blessed encourage ment to keep you inspired to climb that mountain of hopelessness and defeat it. Its my hope to bless each reader with joy, hope, and love.

Printed in the United States
By Bookmasters